Camille Thurman

Sonny Rollins

Grace Kelly

Ben Webster

Wayne Shorter

Ornette Coleman

Paul Desmond

Jason Marshall

Vi Redd

Stan Getz

Lester Young

Cannonball Adderley

Dexter Gordon

Charlie Parker

THE STORY OF THE SAXOPHONE

BY

LESA CLINE-RANSOME

ILLUSTRATED BY

JAMES E. RANSOME

Coleman Hawkins

HOLIDAY HOUSE • NEW YORK

For James "J.E." Williams, Jr., who brings music to our family and our lives. —L.C.-R.

In memory of my buddy Floyd Cooper (Januray 8, 1956–July 15, 2021) —J.R.

Text copyright © 2023 by Lesa Cline-Ransome

Illustrations copyright © 2023 by James E. Ransome

All Rights Reserved

HOLIDAY HOUSE is registered in the U.S. Patent and Trademark Office.

Printed and bound in October 2022 at C&C Offset, Shenzhen, China.

First Edition

1 3 5 7 9 10 8 6 4 2

www.holidayhouse.com

Library of Congress Cataloging-in-Publication Data

Names: Cline-Ransome, Lesa, author. | Ransome, James, illustrator.

Title: The story of the saxophone / by Lesa Cline-Ransome ; illustrated by James E. Ransome.

Description: First edition. | New York : Holiday House, 2023. | Audience: Ages 6–9 | Audience: Grades 2–3

Summary: "The award winners behind Before She Was Harriet explore the story of the saxophone, from its
beginnings in 1840s Belgium all the way to New Orleans, where an instrument in a pawn shop caught the eye of musician
Sidney Bechet and became the iconic symbol it is today"–Provided by publisher.

Identifiers: LCCN 2022035471 | ISBN 9780823437023 (hardcover)

Subjects: LCSH: Sax, Adolphe, 1814–1894–Juvenile literature. | Saxophone—History—Juvenile literature.

Classification: LCC ML3930.S29 C54 2023 | DDC 788.7/19–dc23/eng/20220729

LC record available at https://lccn.loc.gov/2022035471

ISBN: 978-0-8234-3702-3 (hardcover)

THE story of the saxophone doesn't begin with Dexter Gordon or
Charlie Parker. This story isn't told by Lester Young and Coleman Hawkins.
It didn't start on a New Orleans street corner with Sidney Bechet.
It began in 1814, far, far away, across the seas, in Dinant, Belgium.

The story began with a young boy named Joseph-Antoine Adolphe Sax, the only son of an instrument maker. Everyone called him Adolphe.

Adolphe was often bored, so he daydreamed, especially when he should have been paying attention. By the time he was ten, he had fallen down a flight of stairs, swallowed a needle, been poisoned three times, nearly drowned, been burned by gunpowder, and been knocked into a coma from a loose roof tile.

But Adolphe was bored and curious and smart, an absolutely wonderful combination for a boy who loved to invent.

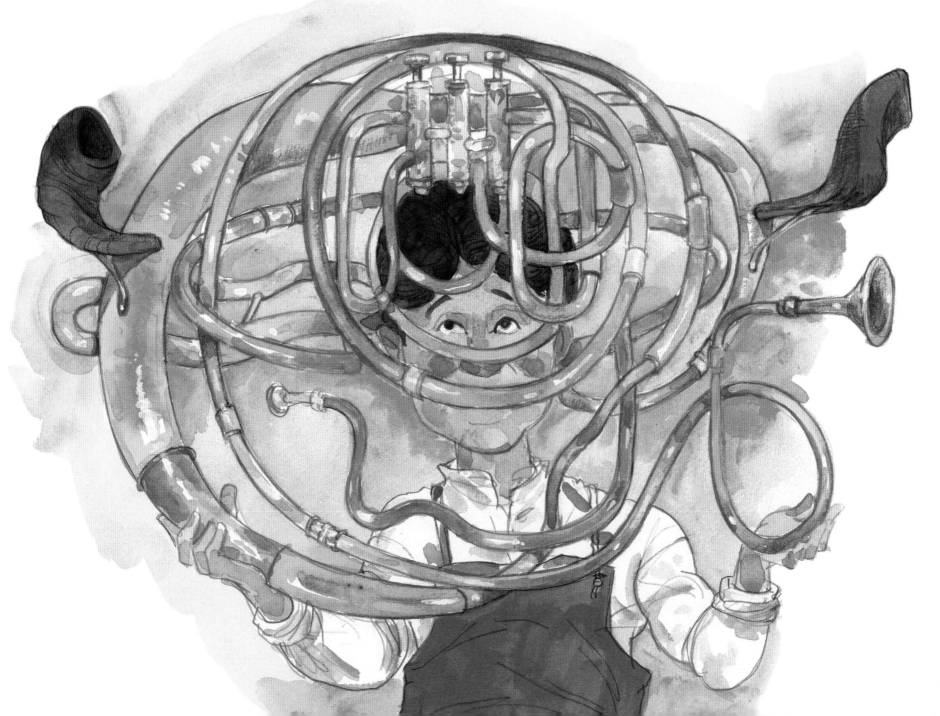

His father let him be while Adolphe tested and tinkered
and tweaked with keys and levers and reeds. Adolphe
played flute, clarinet, and nearly every instrument you
can imagine, including his own creations—the steam
organ, the sax tuba, the sax trombone, the euphonium,
the bass tuba, and the flugelhorn.

But Adolphe was daydreaming of a new sound. Just the right sound. Adolphe had listened to symphonies and marching bands with their grand brass sections, whimsical woodwinds, and lyrical strings.

He knew that they needed an instrument that was not as loud as a trumpet. Not as soft as a clarinet. Somewhere right in the middle.

He assembled one crazy contraption after the next.
Some made sounds that were too tinny. Others too bold.
He added a reed and a mouthpiece. A neck and a body.
A thumb hook and a bell. He listened and played, took
notes, took it all apart and started again. Finally, he
was done.

With one long breath, Adolphe blew into the mouthpiece, and his instrument came to life. It played the high, sweet notes of a clarinet with the deep, low tones of a trumpet and the delicacy of a violin. It was his masterpiece.

Except the judges at the Belgian National Exhibition didn't agree. One competitor kicked Adolphe's masterpiece across the floor.

Adolphe carefully wrapped his dented
invention, packed a few belongings and all
the money he had, and boarded a train to Paris.

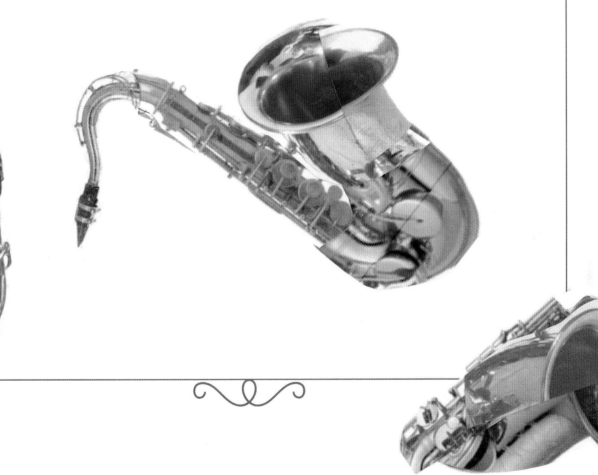

Parisians knew their food and their art, their fashion and their wine, and they certainly felt they knew more about music than this young boy from Belgium. And so, in Paris, the city of love, everyone hated Adolphe and his crazy new instrument.

Everyone, that is, except for his friend, the famous composer Hector Berlioz. When he heard Adolphe play his newest invention, he proclaimed to his audiences, "It cries, sighs, and dreams." He renamed Adolphe's masterpiece *le saxophon*.

Adolphe wanted his instrument in French military bands. Friends helped him play his saxophon for the royal court, and they agreed to let him try out his instrument, as only the French would, in a duel.

A musical duel between the French military band and a band with Adolphe's saxophons. On the day of the duel, several in Adolphe's band were bribed to stay home. A few more never arrived, so Adolphe strapped two saxophons to his neck and joined the band.

The addition of Sax's new instruments made every other instrument sound better. By the end of the first round, the crowd burst into cheers for Adolphe's band.

Within months, the saxophons were a part of every regimental band in Paris. When word of these new saxophons reached Prussia, they insisted Sax make more for their bands. And when Italy, Spain, and Hungary heard about these serpentine saxophons, they placed their orders.

FRANCE

PRUSSIA

ITALY

SPAIN

HUNGARY

25

Some were suspicious of this instrument that curved like a snake and made the seductive sounds of a human voice. They called it a devil's horn. Though finally, much of the world saw the genius of Adolphe Sax. But bad luck still seemed to follow him.

Jealous competitors sued, workers blackmailed him, tools were stolen, his workshop burned to the ground, a bomb was placed under his bed, and he narrowly escaped a stabbing. He developed a tumor on his lip so large he could no longer eat.

His tumor was cured. He rebuilt his factory. His family of saxophons grew—soprano, sopranino, alto, tenor, baritone, bass, fourteen in all. By now, Adolphe's sax was popular in England, Portugal, Russia, Spain, Switzerland, Turkey, and his native Belgium. He was a famous genius. But being famous didn't help his bank account. Finally, he gave over his factory to his sons and sold off his collection of instruments and tools.

Emperor Napoleon III loved music, especially Adolphe's saxophon. When the French went to war with Mexico in 1861, the Emperor brought the French military band with him to Veracruz. The French army lost one battle, won another. But the French military band and its saxophons were the real victors. They played at every battle, wailing in defeat, lifting spirits, rousing troops, shouting victory, until the French lost the war.

Florencio Ramos, a member of the Mexican Cavalry Band, heard those French saxophons. He got his hands on one and later traveled across the gulf to New Orleans to the World's Industrial and Cotton Centennial Expo in 1884. New Orleans had jazz, a new music, from Africa, Europe, and America, pieced together like the parts of a saxophon. Ramos decided to stay in the city filled with music.

Adolphe passed away in 1894, but in New Orleans and other cities, his saxophon lived.

On street corners and in juke joints, at funerals and in jazz clubs, the sound of the saxophon spread to every corner of New Orleans. Only now people called it the saxophone. One day, when a New Orleans clarinetist named Sidney Bechet picked up a saxophone that blew low and slow, just how he liked it, he put down his clarinet and never picked it up again.

And Lester Young heard Coleman play.

Coleman Hawkins heard Sidney play.

And Charlie Parker heard Lester play.

And Dexter Gordon heard Charlie play. And everyone heard Dexter play the saxophone, that began far, far away, across the seas, in a workshop in Belgium, made by a boy everyone called Adolphe.

Booker Ervin

John Coltrane

Chris Potter

Tia Fuller

Branford Marsalis

Joshua Redman

Johnny Hodges

Rahsaan Roland Kirk

Lakecia Benjamin